Riad Sattouf

ESTHER'S NOTEBOOKS

Tales from my 11-year-old life

Translated from the French by Sam Taylor

PUSHKIN PRESS

Back to School

My name is Esther and I'm 10 years old. I'm in Year 6 at a private school in Paris.

This is me and my best friend Cassandra at break time

Life at school is very different this year.

Most of the students are new

There are three groups in my class now. The "runts", the "normals" and the "bad boys".

Me and Cassandra are "normals": we play games and we use swear words, but not all the time.

SHIIIIT! I messed up!

Yup

The "runts" of the class are the ones who are, you know, a bit strange. Like Mitchell, for example.

He still stares out at the street and now he wears his hair in a ponytail sometimes, even though he's a boy

His trousers are still too short

There's also Marina, who spends all her time playing with an imaginary friend.

We'll be playing and she'll wander off, talking to herself

Yes Hector, let's go see Dad ...

Us in "what the...?" mode

And then there's Arthur who's, like, mentally handicapped or something.

This is the movement his mouth makes over and over again all day long (you can't make fun of him or laugh because it's sad)

PWUH

① ② ③

The "bad boys" are a group of kids who have loads of lovers and use loads of swear words. Everybody else wants to be like them (except me).

Lucas, their leader

Cool-dude hand movements

Louis, my ex-husband

Yep, girls can be bad boys too

This is Lina

And guess what! Eugenie, my ex-best friend, is now one of the bad kids. She's Lucas' girlfriend!

They talk in show-off voices

An' then, right, he sez, "Yo, your mother's a ho," and I'm like "You fucking what, dickhead? What didja say?"

Go on, say it again, prick!

It's weird, Eugenie didn't use to care about love at all but now she's obsessed (it's because she's got breasts, I think).

But we're not allowed to use phones – the teacher will tell you off, yo

HAHA who gives a fuck? Screw that, ho

I could never swear like that

I don't know if you remember Maxime, the rich kid who was the most popular boy in school last year? He fell off a rock in Corsica this summer and spent two months in hospital.

He was like this in Year 5

Now he's like this

He used to be the coolest dude and now he's one of the runts. Crazy, huh?

Nobody talks to him any more

He just sits there hugging himself, staring at the others and smiling

(Based on a true story told by Esther A, who is 10 years old)

Riad Sattouf

Chouchous

This week, we chose our chouchous for the year.

This is me getting my hair braided by Cassandra

A chouchou is a scrunchy

But that's not the kind of chouchou I mean

Every year, new Year 2 kids join the school.

Ha ha, look at them!

They're all really tiny, so they're scared of everything.

They cry because they miss their parents or something

And the boys like to beat them up for no reason.

OWW!

WHAT THE HELL! WHY DID YOU DO THAT?

DO WHAT? I DIDN'T TOUCH HIM!

UGH

So the school encourages the bigger kids (Year 5 and Year 6) to choose a chouchou — a favourite — that they can protect and teach about life and stuff.

This is us deciding which ones to choose

So I chose this really cute little girl, and you know what she said to me when I told her she was going to be my chouchou?

Like a little doll

I DON'T WANT TO BE YOURRR CHOUCHOU, I WANT TO BE HERRR CHOUCHOU BECAUSE HER HAIRRR IS SO BEAUTIFUL!

It was the best day of Cassandra's life.

LA LA LA

They're inseparable now

So in the end I didn't choose a chouchou, the teacher gave one to me. Her name is Gwenaelle.

Esther's granny is from Brittany, just like you!

Gwenaelle used to be in a "Diwan" school, where they speak Breton.

Hi there! Welcome to Paris!

Look at her hoodie!

ESTHER! TE ZO KEN KOANTIG HAG UR GALON!

SOMEBODY SAVE ME PLEASE

(Based on a true story told by Esther A, who is 10 years old)

Riad Sattouf

4

Joy

I'm a pretty good student (not the best, not the worst, but better than average).

You know what I don't think people talk about enough? Joy.

Joy is simple: it's when life gives us pleasure and we feel good. It's the best thing ever.

My dad makes me joyful. When he looks at me, I know everything is going to be okay.

For example, here, he's letting me use his iPhone and I go on Wikipedia (a site that knows everything there is to know) to find out if Jupiter (the planet) is made of rocks or gas.

Last time at my dance class we did a routine to "Avenir" by Louane (a singer I like, except for her nose).

I was singing and dancing and doing my moves...

...and I was so good, I was like a professional or something...

The other day, there was some apple juice in the fridge. My mum told me to finish it because she'd opened it two weeks ago and she was worried it would go bad.

I drank the whole thing! My mum thought it was just a mouthful, but it was nearly a litre.

Joy isn't always just a good feeling. For example, when my brother starts insulting me and my dad shuts him up with a look and a single word.

(Based on a true story told by Esther A, who is 10 years old)

Riad Sattouf

5

Teeth

I'm 10 years old and I've already lost 21 teeth!

This is me with my teeth on my chest (my dad keeps some of them in a box at my granny's house)

Teeth are hard white things that grow in your mouth. You use them to eat (and smile).

Yep, this little thing was in my mouth and now it isn't (and yep, nobody cares except my dad)

When you're a child, you have milk teeth and they fall out one by one and other teeth replace them.

This horrible photo of me is from a long time ago. Please don't show it to anybody

I'm always losing my teeth in weird ways (typical me).

One day I was drinking through a straw and watching a film and I accidentally got my tooth caught in the straw

You think that Shrek is your true love?

It was stuck in there so hard, I couldn't get it out again after!

Well... yes! Ha ha ha ha ha ha!

Another time, I was reading a book at my granny's house and my mum gave me a surprise kiss (we do that in our family – my mum's idea)...

Another time, I gave my dad a kiss that made a PFRTTT noise on his belly...

And another time, my brother knocked me out of the hammock in my grandmother's garden...

WHAAT? I'M ALLOWED IN THE HAMMOCK TOO!

I really like my new teeth. They have these little waves on them.

I'm a bit tense here because I'm at the dentist. I'm not scared of her though – she never hurts me and she's really pretty too. Anyway, this is what she said:

Your canines are a little too friendly with your lateral incisors! We're going to have separate them a bit

So I'm going to have a thing on my teeth like my ugly brother.

Heyy, Esther's got braces! Ha ha you're going to SUFFER now bee-yitch!

The dentist told me "Come back in June so I can fit it." Since then, I pray (yes, pray!) to God every night, asking him to take pity on me.

Dear Lord, it's fine to make me suffer because I'm not afraid of suffering. But please please don't let the braces make me uglier than I am. Also, next year I go to secondary school, and if I could stay just a teeeensy bit popular, that would be really great...

(Based on a true story told by Esther A, who is 10 years old)

Riad Sattouf

Les Marseillais

I love the weekend. You can relax, have some time to yourself, and hang out with friends away from school in "no stress" mode.

This is my mum

And me

Cassandra's mum

See you tonight!

My best friend Cassandra

I love Cassandra and I feel so bad for her. Her dad died last year and her mum is poor.

But despite all that, she laughs and sings and enjoys life

YAYY

Oreos, yum!

I would just cry all day if my dad died.

It makes me want to be super-loving with her

Your bedroom is great

Cassandra's mum asked my mum if Cassandra could stay with us on Saturday afternoons while she was working in a shop.

Cassandra is a pretty good student but she doesn't like to read. I'm the opposite – reading is my passion

I should pass it on to her

When she's at home, she watches television all day (she loves reality TV shows).

How about we read "The Baby-Sitters Club"? It's really good

Ugh, no, let's just watch "Les Marseillais"

I'm not allowed to watch TV...

Who cares? We can watch it on my phone ha ha ha

"Les Marseillais" is a programme about real people who want to work in nightclubs and stuff, and they're all from a city called Marseille.

The people in that city have a weird way of talking

C'MON EH!

NAH

For example, they say "Watchatelliimeh" instead of "What did you tell him?" It's hard to understand, but it's still very interesting because it's about "youth" issues.

I'd like him to esplain why he kissed Rawell

Watwazatabouteh?

But he won't tell me

The boys are really sporty and they're always in "chill" mode.

And they're always in their underwear – mmm (just kidding)

C'MON EH

Nah I toldja

Cassandra's favourite is a beautiful girl who's Renoi (that means "black") like her. She's a booking agent or something. She's in charge of the show – she gives the candidates jobs, and sometimes she fires them.

OMG she's so beautiful

You're fired – leave now

So anyway we were watching it and then my mum came in and she talked to Cassandra.

You know, reading is really great! The words conjure images and sounds in your head... Don't you want to put your phone down and use your imagination?

Not really, thanks

On TV there are images and words... In books, there are just words, so many words. That's why I prefer TV. Sorry. I'm just really not interested in imagining stuff. I'd rather SEE it.

I'll be honest: Cassandra is right about the images and the sound and all that. TV is better than books. But when you're not allowed to watch it, like me, then you're really thankful that books exist...

(Based on a true story told by Esther A, who is 10 years old)

The Election

I'm going to tell you about the election of our class delegates.

This is me when I found out that there was going to be an election that afternoon (I was happy because it meant no work)

YAYY!

Elections are democracy. That means that each of us has to write the name of the candidate they like best on a bit of paper and the one with the most votes is "elected" (that means chosen).

In order to ensure the neutrality of the election, the candidates will be anonymous. Everybody will have a chance

Delegates are students who represent the other students and help them talk to the teacher and the headmaster or something.

So each candidate will write a manifesto and I'll read them out

You'll vote for the speech you like best. The words are more important than the people

So everybody who wanted to wrote a little speech and put it in a box with a hole at the top.

I didn't bother – I'd rather be free

Plus I'm a bit of a loner and a dreamer

The teacher read out the speeches. There was a bit of everything...

"If you vote for me, I promise to do all I can to get us some football goals with real nets, and for people who prefer basketball, a new net for the hoop..."

Definitely a boy

It's funny – some of them really want to get elected but they don't actually promise anything.

"Please vote for me! If you vote for me, I'll be so happy, so please will you please vote for me? Please. Thank you."

One of the speeches said: "A vote for me is a vote for pizza" because he was going to ask for pizza four times a week at the cafeteria. Everybody wanted to vote for that one!

The teacher said "That's not going to happen"

HEY what about democracy, miss?

It was his speech

What a joke! Seriously, what's the point?

Lucas said in his speech, "If I'm the delegate, I'll share my cards with all of you..."

He made a little sign so that everybody would know it was his speech. The cheat!

He means his Yu-Gi-Oh! cards

Everybody saw him, and since he's very rich, everybody voted for him to get some cards. But when he realized he was going to get elected, he said this:

Well actually I don't have enough cards for everybody, so I'm not going to give them out. But thanks for voting for me!

What a scam!

The teacher let him get away with it. She said: "It was an electoral promise, you believed it, you voted, end of story."

HE CHEATED MISS! HE SAID WHO HE WAS!

didn't see anything!

I'M GOING TO TELL MY MUM!

The other speech that was elected was a speech that said, "Vote for me and I'll use your ideas, I'll listen to you, and I'll fight for us to be allowed to wear uniforms and stuff..." I voted for that one (uniforms are cool).

And in fact it was a girl called Athena who everybody hates!!!

She's really the worst: she looks like a boy, and when people ask her if she's an intellectual or something, she says "yes"! Honestly, it was horrible when we realized that she was the delegate.

Everybody started booing but it was too late

She smiled like this

(Based on a true story told by Esther A, who is 10 years old)

Riad Sattouf

Electoral Fraud

There are problems with the class delegates at the moment.

This is me listening to Lucas, one of the delegates, telling people his ideas

I'm going to ask for the playground to be named after Aime Jacquet because he coached the French team that won the World Cup in 98, yo

Yeah man GREAT idea

Lucas lied and cheated to become a delegate, so Mathis (the candidate who wanted pizza four times a week) told his mum.

She asked to see the headmaster right away

Madame

She made an official complaint about electoral fraud and demanded new elections.

The headmaster refused because there was no proof of cheating (even though it's true – I saw him cheating!)

Hee hee

Mathis cried

The other delegate is this HORRIBLE girl. She won because the candidates were all anonymous. She's a very ugly person, on the outside AND the inside.

She promised to use our ideas, to look after us, and to ask for school uniforms "like in Japan"

When we found out it was her, we were all really upset

Of course, she didn't do any of the stuff she said she would. All she did was talk to the teacher and the headmaster and she never told us what they talked about! And we elected her!

And not only that, but look at her feet!

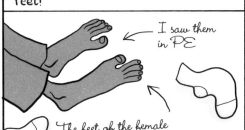

I saw them in PE

The feet of the female chimpanzee at the zoo are better than these, because, you know, at least they're _supposed_ to be hands

At our school there are loads of love affairs. That's just how it is. We get married, we get divorced, we laugh and we cry – that's life, right? The teachers don't like it, but they don't do anything about it. So Athena, instead of asking us for our ideas or campaigning for uniforms like she said she would, told the headmaster that the students had complained to her about the weddings, and that's NOT TRUE – she doesn't talk to any of us and we don't talk to her! So after that meeting with the "educationary staff" or whatever (the teachers, basically), she came out and said THIS:

Okay, so I've arranged it with the headmaster: no more weddings or love affairs. It's age-inappropriate and it's a disruptive influence.

From now on, love is forbidden.

Honestly, if she died right now and somebody told me, "Hey did you hear, Athena is dead?", I reckon I'd say, "Oh yeah?" and I'd go off to play Kemps (it's a card game).

(Based on a true story told by Esther A, who is 10 years old)

Riad Sattouf

Paul and Arthur

I think French is okay as a subject. We should do more of it instead of maths, etc.

This is me being bored at school (even though I'm a pretty good student)

Right now, we're studying the lives of Rimbaud and Verlaine (two poets who lived in the past).

Rimbaud, very good-looking and short-tempered, wrote his first poems at about 15 (five years older than me)

Verlaine, less good-looking (ugly, in fact) and bald, with cruel eyes

They were in love (even though they were both "men") but the teacher doesn't go into details (she doesn't like talking about love).

How would you describe the relationship between Verlaine and Rimbaud?

GAY, YO!

Our teacher (practically a dwarf)

Everybody laughed, then the teacher said, "Yes, but above all it was loving, free, artistic and passionate." Just then, Kalila put her hand up and said:

Um, miss, you shouldn't be talking about homos in school. Sorry, but I think that's shocking

In fact, Verlaine couldn't choose between his wife and Rimbaud (yep, Verlaine was married with a daughter AND he had a boyfriend — weird, huh?) and that made him violent.

Are you okay, mi amore? You don't look well...

Ha ha

Hmph

Pauul! Mwaah

Oh, and we have to learn this poem, but it's really hard:

My Bohemian

I went away, pockets ripped and filled with my fists;
Even my overcoat less real than ideal;
I passed under skies, Muse! And I was yours, feal;
And I dreamed the most wondrous loves that exist!

A hole in my trousers and holes in my sleeves,
Like a dreamy Tom Thumb, sowing rhymes as I roamed,
Sleeping under the sky, Ursa Major my home,
The stars above softly rustling like leaves

And I lay down by roadsides, looked up and listened,
All those sweet September evenings as I felt the dew glisten
On my forehead, like a rough and earthy wine;

There, amid wild fantastic shadows, I made rhymes,
And plucked at the elastics of my ruined shoes like lyres,
One foot close to this beating heart of mine.

Arthur Rimbaud

Actually, it sounds like homosexuality was frowned upon back then just like it is now.

Excuse me, miss, but why are we talking about them? Couldn't we talk about poets who loved girls?

Seriously, I think it's kind of sad to talk about queers all the time

This is Lucas (he's a rebel)

So the teacher stopped talking about that.

Although she did tell us that Verlaine shot Rimbaud and they never saw each other after that

BANG

Rimbaud's hand was messed up

I'm not sure I really understand it, but I like the way it sounds...

... although I don't get what it has to do with a Bohemian, which is a kind of sweater

After the incident with his hand, Rimbaud stopped writing and wandered around the world like a tramp.

He begged on the street like one of those zombies outside the supermarket and nobody knew he was famous!

Have you perchance a few euros so I may eat?

Apparently it didn't work too well

He sold arms to Arabs or something and then his knee hurt and it turned out he had knee cancer (yes, it exists) and they had to cut off his leg.

And then he died in poverty

Actually, my knee hurts too when I do that

I was scared but the doctor said it was "growing pains"

(Based on a true story told by Esther A, who is 10 years old)

Riad Sattouf

The Baby

Do you remember how I told you my mum was pregnant?

This is me putting my glass on her belly because it's funny

Take that off me

LOL

Well, this week, she gave birth! It's weird though: I felt sure I was going to have a sister, but in fact the opposite happened.

We went to see them in the maternity ward (that's the part of the hospital where babies come out of bellies).

MAT

← My dad brought some chocolate-covered pistachios

My mum said the birth went well (it's because this is her third time and she's used to it) but she looked pretty tired.

The baby wasn't with my mum, he was in a little box at the end of the room

We walked over and I saw him!

Gaetan, my little brother

His hair is so blond it looks like it's made of gold and there's loads of it (rare for a baby, apparently)

He's tiiiiny!

This is him awake (his eyes look kind of Chinese but they're super-blue)!

His hands are really perfect and his fingernails are almost microscopic

He's sleeping here. He doesn't move, which is scary, but Mum says it's normal

We were all like this once

When he cries he's really ugly and he sounds like a puppy!

Pretty chubby

His feet look like they're made out of plastic

Prrrpffprrr

He purrs like a cat!

This is his normal expression, with his tongue hanging out like it's too big to fit in his mouth! Will he always look like that?

His mouth is unbelievable

(Based on a true story told by Esther A, who is 10 years old)

Riad Sattouf

A Choice of Fathers

So now I have two brothers! There are five of us in the house.

This is me

It feels weird saying "I have two brothers" because the second one's only just been born

His name is Gaetan

I'd love to have a child of my own.

My dad could crush his skull just by closing his hand

I can tell I'd be really good at looking after a baby.

Can I wear these gloves to change him so I don't get dirty?

NO!

I really adore my mum, but it's weird, I feel like she has nothing in common with my dad.

Hey calm down I was KIDDING!

She never gets my jokes

It's encouraging that somebody like her managed to find a man to have children with.

My feet were never on the grooouuund! If only I were a bird instead ohooooooohhh I don't belong in this body no

A song by Balavoine (an unknown singer) that I love to hum

I don't like Year 6 because nobody plays games any more.

At break time, the girls just wander around the playground and talk

Yeah, right?

Yeah

My ex-friend Eugenie

All they ever talk about is "who loves who" and "who's going out with who"...

And then he said "Yo, I love you"

What? Seriously?!

It gets boring after a while

And, you know, she didn't say anything because she doesn't want to be like "Yeah I'm sooo in love"

So I prefer to just sit in a corner on my own, with my three lovers (yep, three).

This is the SOS of an earthling in distress

They don't know there are three of them. They're all in different classes. One of them plays basketball.

That's him

The second one plays football with the third one.

They don't know they're right next to each other!

We never talk but we smile at each other and we know we're united by love.

I find it reassuring to know I have a choice of fathers. You know, for when I decide I want children.

(Based on a true story told by Esther A, who is 10 years old)

Riad Sattouf

Friday 13th November, 2015

Yesterday was Friday 13th. Apparently that's an unlucky day. My brother told me that there's even a horror film called that (a horror film is a film where loads of people are killed — I've never seen one). But I'm the opposite. I have the feeling that Friday 13th brings me good luck. Last night, my parents were watching a football match on TV (I hate football) and I was in my bedroom. I went to the kitchen to get a drink and when I arrived in the living room my dad turned off the TV and said, "Hey, why don't we watch 'Tangled'" (which used to be my favourite ever Disney film!). So we put it on.

(Based on a true story told by Esther A, who is 10 years old)

Riad Sattouf

Fear

When I got to school on Tuesday, everybody was really frightened.

It happened the night we watched "Tangled".

Terrorists are stupid idiots (sorry to be rude) who kill people that haven't done anything wrong.

I don't understand why they do that. I heard that terrorists are happy to die because they believe that there are women waiting in heaven to make food for them or something.

It's hard to believe anybody could do such a terrible thing.

If they want to commit suicide so they can go to heaven, why don't they just do it in their bedroom? I don't understand why they kill other people too.

And the innocent people they killed hadn't even made fun of the terrorists' god like they did last time with the Charlie.

Afterwards, everybody told stories about people they knew whose lives had been saved by their smartphones.

And then something totally freaky happened to me and Cassandra.

After he left, we just cried and cried.

(Based on a true story told by Esther A, who is 10 years old)

Riad Sattouf

* See Esther's Notebooks: Tales from my 10-year-old life

Secours Populaire

Panel 1
On the last day before the Christmas holidays, the teacher took us to a charity shop called Secours Populaire...

This is me laughing at how small Madame Rodriguez is
This is her – she really is tiny
We were on an outing

Panel 2
We each had to take one of our old toys so they could be given to a poor child.

I brought my Cicciobello...
Really? You didn't want to keep it?
It's a doll that talks if you put batteries in it
Pfft, it's a baby toy!

Panel 3
Secours Populaire is a charity where "volunteers" (people who aren't paid) work to help the needy.

I've got a little brother now so I don't need a doll
Anyway it's broken

Panel 4
The teacher is always talking to us about "all-true-ism", which means being nice and thinking about other people and helping those who aren't as lucky as us or something.

So the teacher gave a speech and so did the people from Secours Populaire, who were all wearing Father Christmas hats, but I didn't actually listen to it

Panel 5
I noticed that the teacher has a stud on her tongue!

Take out your toys now and put them on the table
Doesn't seem very "all-true" to pierce your tongue, but whatever

Panel 6
So anyway, when I put my Cicciobello on the table, she talked (the batteries still worked)!

SCHKRRR YUM YUM MAMA HUUUG KRRR

Panel 7
And then, well, I just burst into tears.

I felt like I was abandoning her or something
Works great – thanks!
KRR MAMA KRR

Panel 8
They gave us each a lollipop then, but since I was crying so hard I couldn't manage to open mine.

I didn't want to admit that I was crying about my doll (what a baby)

Panel 9

Waaaaaah
MPF MPF MPF

Panel 10
When the grown-ups saw me, I became the chouchou of Secours Populaire.

It's okay, love, we'll help you!
What's up?
It's not worth crying over!

Panel 11
And in fact it took all four of them to open it because the plastic was stuck.

They shouldn't make 'em so hard to open
Sniff
There!
How are kids supposed to manage that?

Panel 12
They managed in the end. It made me feel so much better that they all helped me. They're really nice people.

Thank you, Secours Populaire sniff

(Based on a true story told by Esther A, who is 10 years old)
Riad Sattouf

15

Binmen

I'm a "family" kind of girl. That means I like relaxing and doing nothing in our little cocoon.

Yep, my mum and dad read books. They have a bookshelf in the corridor, but they're all adult books (horror and politics, stuff like that).

My brother Antoine doesn't read, he just looks at his phone.

HEY, I _do_ read! I read loads of websites, yo

Don't say I don't read

My brother is such a thug

I read!

I'm really into reading this year. It all began with "Little Women", which my granny bought for me.

It's the story of four sisters, their mother and their faithful servant who try to manage while the father is out at the war being a doctor

Farewell my daughters, duty calls...

My favourite character is Jo March because she's fearless and she has long black hair like me.

I WANT TO GO TO WAR TOO! BUT I CAN'T BECAUSE I'M A WOMAN! IT'S NOT FAIR!

Come on Jo, why don't you help me make dinner instead?

I also really like "The Baby-Sitters Club". It's a series about some girls who form a club for babysitters and it works well and then they have adventures and help each other when they have problems looking after the kids.

I have a little brother, so I can relate to that

Hold him — he might fall off!

The character I like best is Kristy Parker. She's great.

I like her name, it just sounds really cool

A rebel

Sporty, casual clothes like jeans and T-shirt, so she's ready for action

Bendy

She's just like me

At school they asked us what we wanted to do when we were older and I said "read books" because I love it so much.

Do you want to write them too?

Nah, not really, just read them...

You're right — writers don't get paid much. You could be an "editor"

REALLY?

Apparently, an editor is somebody who chooses what books to publish and sometimes you even give orders to writers so they write what you want, and then you sell them and you can get very rich! Sounds AMAZING, right?

I want your novels by tonight.

YES BOSS

Oh, and Lucas said "binman" for a joke and everybody laughed and the teacher said we mustn't make fun of binmen because without them we'd be drowning under rubbish and besides it was very well paid because of the bad smells and stuff (3,000 euros).

YO, 3,000 EUROS?

After that, everybody said, "We want to be binmen," because they thought they only worked in the mornings...

They wake up VERY EARLY, so their hours are as long as everyone else's

HEY for 3,000 euros I'd wake up early miss

And then I had an idea for a novel with a bin-girl who's also a detective because she finds clues in the rubbish, and she's the only girl in a team of men (I don't know where I get all these ideas).

(Based on a true story told by Esther A, who is 10 years old)

Riad Sattouf

Imaginary Books

I love my dad but he's very strict: he won't let me have a smartphone and doesn't like it when I watch TV. On the other hand, he loves it when I read books. As soon as I finish one, I'm allowed to get a new one right away (no need to wait for my birthday or Christmas or whatever). We go to a bookshop where there's loads of choice and I can choose whatever I want. Now I don't know if this is the fault of the bookshop (for choosing the wrong books) or the writers (for writing bad books), but I have to say there are a lot of boring-rubbish-not-very-interesting books that I don't want to read at all. So here are a few ideas for books that, if they existed, I would want to read (LOL):

"A young girl kills herself because the girls at school make fun of her. Then she comes back to haunt them and takes her revenge on them, one by one..."
(Horror/Suspense)

THE YOUNG DEAD GIRL

The Popular Girls Club

"Some pretty, popular girls start a club to help ugly girls get over their problems and they have lots of adventures..."
(Action/Advice)

The Secret Diary of a GIRL IN LOVE

"A diary that reveals ALL the author's secrets about love..."
(Romance/Reality)

"The story of a girl who has never seen her father, only an old black-and-white photo of him, so she goes in search of the man he was..."
(Drama)

A GIRL WITH NO FATHER
ESTHER A.

Always useful, right? (Kidding)
(Guide)

500 IDEAS FOR Romantic LETTERS TO MAKE HIM love you

THE DEFINITIVE GUIDE TO DISCREET MAKE-UP

Because I love wearing make-up but I don't like it when it's too obvious!
(Techniques/Tips)

"A girl wakes up one morning and all the men on earth have disappeared! Happy days!"
(Humour)

Esther and THE WORLD WITHOUT MEN

(Based on a true story told by Esther A, who is 10 years old)

Riad Sattouf

The Crystal Ball

(Based on a true story told by Esther A, who is 10 years old)

Riad Sattouf

The Journalist

This week, I turned eleven! Did you know that for the past year I've been telling stories about my life to a friend of my dad's who works as a cartoonist?

Yeah, I've got three boyfriends at the same time...

This is me telling him about my life

For my birthday, the cartoonist gave me the book of cartoons that he'd made from my stories.

I don't read many cartoon books. I prefer novels like "The Baby-Sitters Club"

But I liked this one because it's all about my life. And it's mostly true.

Except the boy in the train station – he kissed me on the cheek, not on my mouth

Actually those cartoons appear in a newspaper (although I can't remember its name, sorry) before they're turned into a book.

There's a journalist from that paper who'd like to interview you

Really? Sure. WHENEVER HE WANTS.

Good plan

My mum wanted us to go to a café, but I didn't want to be alone with a stranger.

So he came to our apartment

Hello

He didn't look anything like a journalist.

He looked more like a singer from the 1960s

Not VERY good-looking, but not ugly either

1960s hairstyle

But I didn't like his clothes at all.

The colours on his sweater didn't go together AT ALL

Jeans were WAY too pale

"Young and trendy" trainers

First he said that we had to sit really far apart.

Was he scared I would eat him or what?

So is it true you like Balavoine?

Then he wanted to know if the pigeon had really been killed, if Eugenie's mum really had enormous breasts, and so on...

Yeah, it's TRUE

He asked me three times if I wasn't tired of the cartoonist calling me.

I mean, I wouldn't want him to call me every day, but...

Then, before he left, I remembered something in the book that wasn't true at all any more, so I told him.

"TANGLED" ISN'T MY FAVOURITE FILM ANY MORE.

THAT'S ALL.

(Based on a true story told by Esther A, who is 11 years old)

Riad Sattouf

The Curse

I don't believe in God at all. Do you?

This is me listening to Cassandra explain to me why I should believe

God created everything!

We're at school

Look at your hand! It's so perfect, how can it not have been designed by someone?

But didn't our parents have the idea of making us?

No, it goes way beyond that! Look at your thumb, how practical it is. Someone had the idea of putting it like that, facing the other fingers. It couldn't just be chance...

Good point

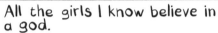

All the girls I know believe in a god.

My friends' god is Jesus Christ

There are loads of different gods. I don't know them all, though, because it's not really my thing.

But I'm listening

He died on a cross, with nails here!

They go to "catchetizum" or something. It's like another school where a man explains "the path of God".

Apparently he says he's in direct contact with God

Jesus tells him what to do with us

He dresses in black

My ex-friend Eugenie practically turned into a teenager this year: she says loads of swear words and she got breasts and a bad-boy lover.

She doesn't talk to me any more

So her parents sent her to catchetizum all through the holidays and she came back, like, totally transformed.

Look at her now

Not showing off any more

She told us that the man of god had placed a CURSE on her because of the sins she'd committed (sins are bad things that you do).

This was the first time she'd talked to us all year!

He said sinners go to hell!

Hell is a place full of flames where people suffer for eternity. That's where the gods send their enemies.

I've done so many bad things.

To lift the curse, Eugenie has to pray a lot and not hang out with bad people and loads of other things.

I'm going to change. Be good.

I think talking to us was one of the things on her to-do list. We walked away.

She can wait for a while in purgatory...

What's that?

Hell's waiting room

(Based on a true story told by Esther A, who is 11 years old)

Riad Sattouf

The Truth About God

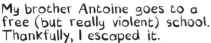

Panel 1: My brother Antoine goes to a free (but really violent) school. Thankfully, I escaped it.

This is me with Cassandra trying to avoid Eugenie in the playground

Let's pretend we haven't seen her

Yeah

Panel 2: I've known Eugenie since we were little, but we haven't talked much since we started Year 6.

Oh yeah, well I think, you know...

Oh really?

Hi there!

Panel 3: She grew breasts and she hung around with the group of "bad boys" (the popular kids).

But when she started getting rebellious, her parents sent her to catchetizum (the school of God)

OH, Eugenie... yes?

I HAVE TO TELL YOU...

Panel 4: Her God-teacher, this man who wears black, put a curse on her and told her that she was going to hell unless she changed.

I said thirty "Our Fathers" every day to get the pardon, yo

IT WAS HARD, MAN

Panel 5: I didn't believe in God, but since all the girls I know do believe – and keep talking about him all the time – I thought, well, maybe he does exist.

I even knelt in front of the cross!

Panel 6: There are too many weird things in nature for them not to have been created by someone.

Who designed the orchid's petals?

Who decided the parrot's beak would look like that?

Who makes sure the patterns are the same on both the butterfly's wings?

Panel 7: Apparently God is a man with a white beard who controls everything (basically he knows everything, sees everything, and hears everything).

He doesn't have a wife but he does have a circle above his head

Very good-looking

Panel 8: He watches what we do from above and he judges us to decide whether we deserve to join him in heaven when we die.

Esther's said "shit" five times this morning... How terribly vulgar...

Hmm...

Panel 9: If we do something bad, he doesn't want us, so he sends us to hell. That's why people are scared of God. I'm scared now too.

Apparently even your eyes burn in hell

... but since you're already dead, you just keep on suffering for ever without dying again

Panel 10: So the priest made the sign of the cross and said "I wash away your sins, my child..."

AND IT'S LIKE HE WASHED AWAY ALL MY BELIEF IN GOD!

Panel 11: His breath smelled really bad, like he'd been eating poo or something...

... and I thought, "Hey, it's all a lie, he's not in contact with God cos if he was, God would say, 'Try brushing your teeth before you wash away people's sins.'"

Panel 12: And that's when I realized that God is just like Father Christmas, HE DOESN'T EXIST! Our parents are just making us believe in him so they can control us.

I HATE THEM!

GEE, THANKS A LOT – JUST WHEN I WAS STARTING TO BELIEVE!

(Based on a true story told by Esther A, who is 11 years old)

Riad Sattouf

Three Lovers

My love life is strange this year. Until this week, I had three lovers at the same time but they didn't know about each other. There was the one who played basketball...

With the basketball player, it was the same — we just smiled from a distance. But then one day he smiled at me AND THEN he came to see me and started doing this "rap-style" version of a song by Oreo Sam or something, and it was crazy.

But, you know, I only laughed. And then my two other lovers stopped playing football and started crying, each in a DIFFERENT CORNER OF THE PLAYGROUND! They couldn't stand it when they saw me laughing at Lover 1's joke!

BOTH THEIR HEARTS HAD BEEN BROKEN AT THE SAME TIME AND FOR THE SAME REASON AND THEY NEVER EVEN KNEW IT! But, you know, why did they never come and talk to me? I was right there, waiting for them.

(Based on a true story told by Esther A, who is 11 years old)

Riad Sattouf

22

The Club

So the reason I go to a private school, according to my beloved father, is that free schools "are shit". Just to be clear, we're not rich. At all.

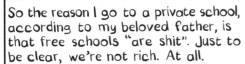

This is me and him in the street (he's protecting me from the zombie guy who always sits in front of the supermarket and scares me)

I'm fairly popular but I'm not the most popular girl in my school because I'm not interested in BRANDS.

Are those Vans... or not?

Well, I'm a little bit interested but I'm not very good at recognizing them

At the start of the year, some of the students started doing bad-boy stuff (talking about sex, swearing, dressing like rappers).

The headmaster summoned the students' parents and said they needed to discipline their children

This is him telling Lucas to pull his trousers up

You could see his boxer shorts

One of the bad boys was a girl called Lina. This is how she used to be:

Yo, whassup?

Lay it on me bro

She called everybody "bro", even other girls

The headmaster talked to her parents

Now she's normal... But she wears a new pair of shoes EVERY DAY.

Platform soles

"Bainmal" boots (or something)

Her sister's "Marc J Cubs" pumps

Her family is, like, super-rich.

I got them for 98 euros on sale in London

She talks to me sometimes

WOW

In other words, even on sale they're way too expensive for someone like me

She even has a pair with a real cartoon strip on them.

I really like this pair

I want them SO much

So the ex-bad boys have now started a club of people who wear white "Stan Smiss" trainers.

Look how white their trainers are

All you need is a pair of Stan Smiss and you can be their friend.

HI!

Hey, I love your 'Stan Smith' Bolds

Even though he's ugly

So anyway, the other day, Lina gave me a pair of hers!

Yo, I don't wear them any more. And they're fakes

OH THANK YOU THAT'S SO KIND

They have a gold strip just here

So I put them on and went to see the members of the club.

HI THERE!

Uh sorry but you can't get in the Stan Smith team with those. They're not real, they're just cheap rip-offs

HA HA

They spotted them from ten feet away! HOW IS THAT EVEN POSSIBLE?

(Based on a true story told by Esther A, who is 11 years old)

Riad Sattouf

23

The Lost Soul

I would say I have a "super-sensitive" personality.

I feel other people's pain. I'm really good at seeing things through their eyes. And it's hard sometimes.

I realized that he was incapable of love. I'd thought he was in love with me but really he was just pretending. It gave me a shock.

Well, I think he _believed_ that his feelings were sincere. We went out together for THREE days. On the first day, a girl came up to me and SLAPPED ME! She was his ex-girlfriend, the one he'd dumped for me. That should have set off alarm bells.

I didn't even realize that, when I thought I was his girlfriend, I was really just playing Cupid for him and Lina! They got married on the afternoon of the day he dumped me.

I wanted to kill her, but then he dumped her for an older girl with a long ponytail... He's got a serious problem. He'll be very unhappy in life if he just goes from girl to girl and never feels anything.

Despite his passion for basketball and his amazing looks (the dark, mysterious type), I have a feeling that life is going to be hard for him.

I really don't know what we can do to help him.

(Based on a true story told by Esther A, who is 11 years old)

Riad Sattouf

24

Reproduction

I have a secret love. His name is Mathis.

This is me gazing tenderly at him

He loves me too

He should have been a delegate but he was cheated of victory

This week, we started learning about "human reproduction", which is basically how babies are "made" in women's bellies.

I've made some reproduction flash cards and we'll go through them together

No, it's not badly drawn: my teacher really is a dwarf or something

---

Before, I used to think that people made babies by hugging.

My parents do a lot of hugging

One day in summer camp, a boy hugged me because we'd won at dodgeball...

YEEAAAH!

That night, I cried because I felt sure I was going to have a baby (I had stomach ache too).

Esther! What's the...

SOORRRY DAAAD I MADE A BABY IN CAAMP!

WAAA

But then I found out how babies were really made by watching Youporn on Eugenie's phone.

I lied last year when I said I didn't go on that site

In fact I did and it was horrible

It shouldn't be allowed

It's this website that shows videos where people make babies by being violent or whatever.

Afterwards we didn't talk because we were so traumatized

And that's the truth

So anyway, the teacher started telling us about reproduction and all that but WITHOUT telling us how it was "done"! WEIRD, RIGHT?

So... Once the man and the woman have... you know... um, well, we're going to study what happens after that

Lots of us didn't know at all

Someone asked how it was "done" and some other people laughed. The teacher told us, "If you want a detailed description, ask your parents". And then Kalila said:

Miss, can I leave the class? It's not right to talk about these things

---

The teacher said "No" and asked if anybody knew what the ovum and spermatozoa were.

Kalila put her hands over her ears (I think it's her God who won't let her discuss this stuff)

Lucas, the class delegate, asked if he was allowed to reply even if the answer was shocking. The teacher said "yes".

The ovum is the girls' egg and the spermatozoa are the little creatures inside men's sperm

Sperm is made in the balls

Everybody started laughing and talking and the teacher told us to calm down. And just then, my lover Mathis turned to me and whispered:

Esther! I've got sperm, you know...

He was, like, bright red

And I was like "?!?!?!?!?!?!?!?!?!"

(Based on a true story told by Esther A, who is 11 years old)

Riad Sattouf

25

Single

So last week we started studying human reproduction.

This is me when Mathis (my secret love) told me he had "sperm"

Umm...

Thankfully the teacher told us all to stop talking, because I had no idea what to say (definitely not age-appropriate).

("Sperm" is like a boy's period, and there are spermatozoa inside it)

So the teacher told us what happened between the spermatozoa and the ovum and all that.

Well... Okay. Let's start

The fertilization of the ovum

Yep, she was embarrassed

In fact, it's really just like life, this whole thing with the spermatozoa and the ovum.

The spermatozoa are the boys...

... and the ovum is the girl

There are billions of spermatozoa swimming as fast as they can into the girl's belly to find the ovum (yep, there's only one ovum).

Quiiick

Where is it?

Psst! Ovum!

And they all fight to be the first one to get there (not surprising – they're boys). And the ovum chooses just one of them to marry (I think she swallows it or something)...

YOU! COME ON!

Argh!

Noooo! Why him, yo?

Fuck, no!

YES

GET IN THERE

Once the ovum has swallowed the spermatozoon she chose, all the others die miserably.

Yep, billions of spermatozoa die all alone each time this happens

Ungh

Then the ovum and her husband go to the Youterrace, which is like an apartment or something inside the woman's belly, and they stay there for nine months.

And that makes a baby which is like a mix of the two parents.

Just an "example"

If the ovum stays alone and no spermatozoa come to see her, well, she dies too in a river of blood.

Uunngh

So being single guarantees you a miserable death

The death of the ovum is called the "period".

Lina, in my class, has had her period, but only once

It's called the "monarch" or something'.

Will I have that too? Ugh!

I hate all these subjects (body – sex – how babies are made, etc.)

I think it's WRONG that we're forced to learn all that when we're not interested!

(Based on a true story told by Esther A, who is 11 years old)

Riad Sattouf

Making Babies

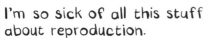

Panel 1:
I'm so sick of all this stuff about reproduction.

This is me writing the word "reproduction"

Our PETITE (that's the right word) teacher

Panel 2:
Esther, write it here! You've still got space at the bottom!

Panel 3:
AHWHAHAHA HAHAHA HAH SPACE AT THE BOTTOM HA HA HAHA HAHAHA HAHA BOTTOM

Panel 4:
All boys are obsessed with sex. It's literally all they think about.

Even Arthur, who's mentally handicapped, is just like the others

BHAHAHA BOTTOM HEE HEE HEE

Panel 5:
The only girl I know who's like that is Louisa, a friend from my dance class. Last year, I invited her to my birthday party and she did this.

Oh Ken oh yesss harder

Stop it! What's wrong with you?

Ken from Ken and Barbie

She's crazy

Panel 6:
I mean, us girls are also interested in love and all that, but only because of the babies we'll have.

I'm going to have a baby on my 13th birthday

OH REALLY?

Well yeah, why wait?

Panel 7:
Cassandra wants a baby too, but she's the opposite of Louisa.

I do want a baby but not until I'm retired.

I want to enjoy life before then.

Panel 8:
I dream of having children, but I'd prefer to get them without having sex or giving birth.

Eugenie told me once that her sister and her sister's boyfriend slept together and she'd heard her sister moaning in pain and the next morning her sister had told her, "Don't worry, we were just having sex"

I was shocked

Panel 9:
Birth is horrible because apparently they give you an injection to take away the pain, and the injection is ten times more painful than giving birth.

Don't move! This may hurt a bit

AGH!

SKWIRT

They stab you in the back!

Panel 10:
I'm still pretty young, though, so maybe they'll come up with a way to make babies remotely in the future?

She looks just like me!

ROBOWOMB 50

And my belly will stay flat (yesss!)

Panel 11:
I saw a cartoon once of a white swan that was vomiting babies out of its beak to give them to women or something.

Whose is this?

Mine! Mine!

Panel 12:
Sorry, I meant a stork, not a swan! Why did I say a swan?!

This was a really good idea

Why isn't life like that?

(Based on a true story told by Esther A, who is 11 years old)

Riad Sattouf

27

The Outing

Last Saturday, Cassandra came to our apartment like she does almost every Saturday.

This is me kissing her on the cheek to say hello

Okay, girls, Marie-Pierre and I have discussed this and we've decided to let you walk around the neighbourhood ON YOUR OWN...

... and here's 5 euros to spend on whatever you want!

It was the first time in my life I'd been allowed out without a grown-up!

We dressed in "sunny day" mode and went out into the street!

(Yep, Cassandra got her hair straightened)

Flower T-shirt

I love these red heart sunglasses, they're really FUN.

They're not a famous brand or anything, just plastic, but they're still cool

The first thing we did was go to the bakery and look at mini-donuts.

5 euros divided by 60 centimes... how many can we get?

HMM!

We bought 8 filled with Nutella (like a really yummy chocolate cream)!

My mum hardly ever gets me donuts, and never more than one

We ate them all and watched the video of "Friend Zone" by Matty B on Cassandra's phone.

We sat on the bench like this

In "do what we want" mode

Matty B is a kid rapper who's really good-looking (like a young Justin Bieber) who made a video where he loves a girl but she thinks of him as just a friend (very funny).

I think we could be

Something like more than just friends

Afterwards we talked about how we might bump into him in the street (yeah, right)!

♪ Mattyyy we're here where are you? ♪ We want to be more than just friends! ♪

Crying with laughter

I yelled that

And then I saw a boy who looked just like him (he was with a Renoi).

They didn't know I was looking at them, because of my glasses

Footballer hair

We were only allowed out for one hour, so we went home and I said to my mum:

Yo, Mum! Can we go out again next week for 2 hours with 20 euros?

Thanks

Her: "..."

So that was my first outing!

(Based on a true story told by Esther A, who is 11 years old)

Riad Sattouf

The Nice Boy

Do you prefer girls or boys? I DEFINITELY prefer girls. We would be perfectly fine without any boys at all. All we need them for is making babies. That's the only useful thing they do. I've had boyfriends of course. But, to be honest, I only loved them for their good looks or their smiles. As soon as we started talking, it was... how can I put this? Just a load of crap, basically. They only like boring things, they're always swearing, and they're way too full of themselves. I have an older brother called Antoine and he's so, sooo stupid. For example, when we sit next to each other on the sofa, if I accidentally touch him, he'll say "Get off me, I'm going to puke!" Isn't that just really stupid and annoying? And, as if that wasn't enough, four months ago, I got ANOTHER brother. But I have to admit, he has changed the way I think about boys a little bit. The other day, my mum was about to take a shower and she put him in my arms and I held him like that. I looked at him and – for the first time ever – he SMILED at me!

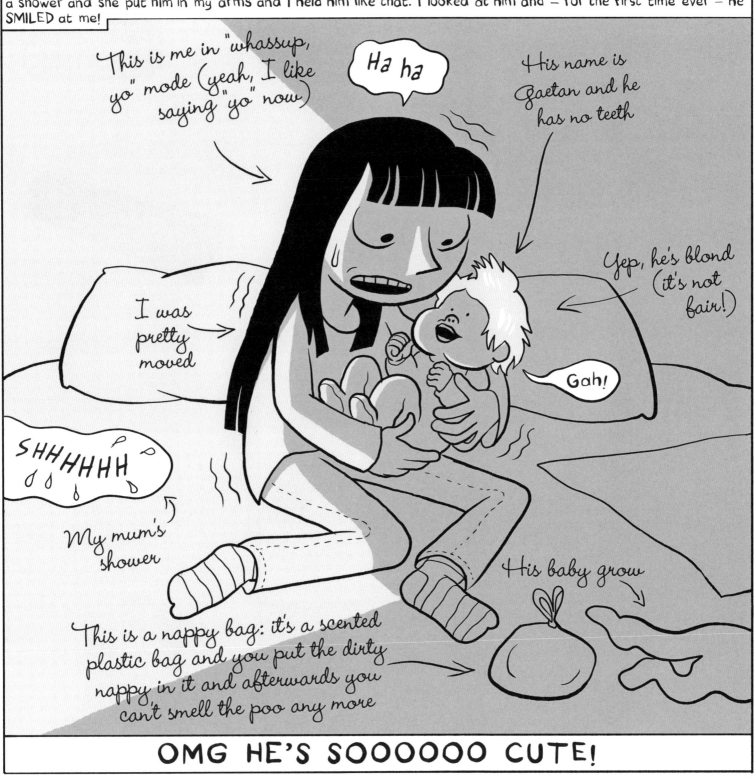

OMG HE'S SOOOOOO CUTE!

(Based on a true story told by Esther A, who is 11 years old)

Riad Sattouf

Passion

I always liked bags, but now I think I'm starting to develop a passion for them.

This is me with my old "Frozen" schoolbag

← I got it in Year 2

I really loved it because I loved the film (I still like it now even if it seems kind of "little-kiddish"), but I don't use it anymore.

Back then I totally identified with Elsa and Anna, the sisters in the kingdom of Arendelle

But now it's over (that's life)

I also had a "Violetta" bag that I don't use any more (I don't watch that show now... well, I do sometimes, but I don't like it as much as I used to).

Nobody has this at my school now →

I really liked that character though

Now I have a simple cloth bag with a flower pattern. It goes well with anything (very practical).

Ideal for shopping with my mum on sunny days

In fact, I like anything that can "contain" stuff or "carry" stuff.

My old "pink shark" pencil case. A bit babyish but I like it

← I used to be crazy about it

Today, this is more my style:

Graffiti-style writing (graffiti is street art that people paint on walls in cities and I love it) →

Everything "real" comes from the street ("real" as in "keeping it real, yo")

In recent years, I've had this pink and green "flower" backpack. Since my parents don't have much money, and I don't want to be a burden on them, I kept it all the way through Year 4 AND Year 5.

It's nice, but the colours are a bit "little girl"

Me, striking a pose (LOL)

But anyway, this year I got sick of it. In fact, Lina – this girl in my class who has a passion for fashion and is very rich (she has a pair of new shoes almost every day) said this to me:

Aren't you sick of that flowery bag? You should get an Eastpak like me. They're not expensive and they're really solid...

Everybody at school has an Eastpak and they're really good, but I always thought they were too expensive. So I asked my dad if I could have one.

Abso FFFF lute FFFF ly FFFF not FFFF

My dad does a lot of exercise

But in the end we went to Go Sport and my dad bought one for me (he can't resist me).

50 euros is expensive! I expect you to keep it ALL the way through secondary school...

I PROMISE, DAD!

Plastic-wrapped

But then I put it on at home and the straps were, like, <u>really stiff</u>, and I started crying.

The horror!

I thought it was broken

It's fiiiine! It's just because it's empty and new... Put a dumbbell inside, you'll see...

I did what he said and it was perfect! →

My dad, the man who solves all my problems →

I LOVE HIM <u>SOOOO</u> MUCH

(Based on a true story told by Esther A, who is 11 years old)

Riad Sattouf

30

Death

I'm going to tell you how I got the biggest fright of my life and how I ended up with 120 euros because of it.

This is me in "pose" mode

My brother Antoine

I don't want to be a vampire!

It was last week. We'd stayed at home and my brother was being weirdly nice.

Chica vaaampiro chica Vam Vam Vaaaam

He'd agreed to watch "Chica Vampiro", a TV series I love

Our parents were in the park with Gaetan. Suddenly there was a knock at the door.

BANG! BANG! BANG!

Did... did you lock it?

Dad told us not to open it

No... Did you?

EEE... KLAK!

The door opened!

And someone came in!

DAAAAD?

Footsteps

TAP
TAP
TAP
TAP

YO, I'M DEATH

My brother jumped up to protect me!

AAAAAAARRRRRGGGGHHH

SO THE KILLER STABBED HIM!

AAAAAAARRRRRGGGGHHH

CHAKK
CHAKK
CHAKK

I screamed at the top of my voice and I turned around and saw Lucien, my brother's friend, take off his mask. And my brother stood up and said:

AAAAAAARRRRRGGGGGHHH

Es... Esther we were just kidding...

Fuck, man, why's she screaming like that?

Afterwards I felt sick. I couldn't breathe and Lucien ran out in tears because he thought he'd killed me.

Esther... Please breathe! I thought it'd make you laugh... Please don't tell Dad — I'll give you all my savings!

HH HH

And suddenly I felt a bit better.

Okay... Give me the money.

I will! Right away...

When my dad came home, I told him what had happened and he said, "Keep the money" and he got really mad at Antoine!

He wanted to report Antoine to the police (LOL)

Antoine cried

I told you he was stupid

My 120 euros

(Based on a true story told by Esther A, who is 11 years old)

Riad Sattouf

31

Lezzer

I've had several boyfriends in my life, but the truth is that I hate boys. They disgust me.

This is me in the playground watching them, a few months ago

The worst boys are the ones who are "girly": they're just like girls, but they're actually boys. I mean, what's the point? I prefer girls.

For example, Mitchell's in Year 6 and at break time he plays with some Year 3 girls (yep, you read that right)!

When another boy calls him a "queer" (that means gay), sometimes he just bursts out crying.

HA HA look at that queer!

WAAAH SNNFF WAAAH

What does "queer" mean?

Fight him, instead of just whining like a girl!

And then there are those really boring boys who just "don't exist". They're not good-looking or ugly, they play football and they swear a lot, but nobody cares about them.

Him, for example

I'm going to fucking cross it!

JUST FUCKING PASS IT

I didn't tell you this, but once, one of those boys fell off a wall and some guys came with an ambulance to take him away.

Move your legs, lad! Don't fall asleep, lad! You hear me? Lad?

I think he might have broken his neck or something...

But at lunchtime, his "friends" just played football as usual, like nothing had happened. They couldn't care less about him!

I wonder if it's almost worse to be that kind of boy than to be like Mitchell

GOOOOAAAALLLL

FUCKING GET IN!

(He did get better btw)

And then there are the bad boys. They're really popular and they only talk about two things: sex and fighting. They're horrible.

An' he wer' like "Fuck yer MOTHER you son of a bitch" an' I said "Whatcha say to me you fucking queer?" an' so anyway I smashed that motherfucking son of a bitch in his fucking mouth

Louis, an ex-boyfriend of mine from Year 5

Sorry for all the swear words but that's the reality of my life

They're really tough. For example, one day Lucas fell over while playing football and injured his face.

Fucking excellent

I FUCKED UP my face, man HA HA!

He didn't cry at all even though he was pouring with blood (I must admit that impressed me a bit. It's, like, superhuman or something)

The other day, when we were talking about how crap boys are, Cassandra (my best friend) said:

You really hate boys, don't you? Maybe you're a lezzer?

"Lezzer" means "gay woman"

My dad has a female cousin who's gay. One day she came to my granny's house with two of her lezzer friends.

Good journey?

God, the traffic jams...

Hello Esther

Honestly, they looked just like men. They really copied their style. What's the point in not loving men if you're just going to look like them?

If I was gay, I'd be super-feminine and I'd only love very very very feminine women (that's just my opinion, sorry if you're offended)

Yo, whas-sup?

She said that even though she's, like, 40 years old!

So I don't like boys, I don't like gay women... I'm going to be single for the rest of my life.

I love Lucas. I was so scared for him when he fell... and he just laughed!

The good news is that I won't be the only one, I think...

(Based on a true story told by Esther A, who is 11 years old)

Riad Sattouf

32

The Attack

My name is Esther, I'm 11 years old and I'm sooo scared. My best friend Cassandra told me that there'd been a terrorist attack in Belgium. She said that actually everybody knew this guy was a terrorist, even the police, but nobody did anything. She said he should really have been in prison but instead he was just free to go wherever he wanted. And then he told the police where he was going and he put the bomb in the metro and it killed loads of people. And Cassandra told me she saw a TV programme that said there were thousands of people just like him all over Europe and that nobody could do anything about it and that it was going to happen again. And then she cried.

This is me and my family (except for my older brother) going for a walk in Bain-de-Bretagne near where my granny lives. Yes, my dad still carries me on his shoulders

My dad's response when I asked him if what Cassandra had told me was true

No *HF!* it's total rubbish *HF!* and just shows *HF!* why you shouldn't *HF!* watch TV *HFFF!*

Oh and we also saw a goat

My dad tries so hard to protect me that it's probably better if I don't ask him stuff any more. Because I can tell it stresses him out to have to lie to me to protect me (and then I get stressed out by seeing him stressed out by having to lie, etc. etc.)

(Based on a true story told by Esther A, who is 11 years old)

Riad Sattouf

The Test

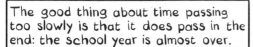

The good thing about time passing too slowly is that it does pass in the end: the school year is almost over.

This is me and Cassandra complaining about the atmosphere at our school

God it's SO boring here

Tell me about it!

We were supposed to go to the same private secondary school next year (Cassandra is very poor but her mum sweats blood to give her a better life) and we were happy about that.

Can't wait till we get out of here...

I know!

But then one evening my beloved father came into my bedroom and this is what he told me:

Esther... We've got less money now that Gaetan is with us... I'm not going to be able to pay for private school any more... You'll have to go to the public school...

in SHOCK

My world collapsed. We'd become even poorer than Cassandra!

I was so sad that I cried my eyes out (it's an expression: my eyes didn't actually pour out of my head)

I don't know what it's like where you live, but in Paris if you want to go to a free school you don't get to choose it – you just have to go to the one closest to your home.

And the one closest to us is really horrible. That's where my brother goes

My brother goes to a ZPEP, which is the official name for a crappy school. It's a dangerous place with loads of violence.

In primary school, my brother was like this:

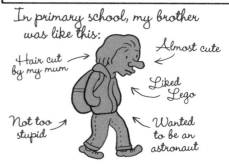

Hair cut by my mum

Almost cute

Liked Lego

Not too stupid

Wanted to be an astronaut

Now he's in a ZPEP:

Wants footballer hair

Really stupid all the time

Go fuck yer fat ho grandma's pussy yo

Says a thousand terrible swear words per minute

Wants to be a rapper

Since I'm a good student, my dad signed me up to take a test. If I pass it, I'll get to go to a much better school in the centre of Paris!

It'll be hard, but you can do it! You have to try!

These schools are in neighbourhoods so expensive that only billionaires can afford to live there, and most of the students are from rich families. They sometimes let in people from other places, but it's really hard. There's an exam and an interview.

It was near the Seine

My dad wasn't allowed to go in.

Be yourself and you'll be fine!

I felt like I was leaving him for ever

I'd never seen such a massive school before. It was like a castle. I got lost. So I went over to this woman who was standing in the courtyard. She was reading a piece of paper. There was nobody else around.

H... Hello... I... I've come to take the entrance exam and... and I don't know where to go...

Oh really? That's lucky – I've come to take the test too! It's Door B3...

Are you telling me this girl is my age?

(Based on a true story told by Esther A, who is 11 years old)

Riad Sattouf

34

Heinrich

Just to remind you, I'm currently in Year 6 at a private school in Paris. But I had a little brother and now we're very poor.

This is me listening to my dad tell me that I'll have to go to a free school next year

I had two choices: go to the same school as my brother Antoine, which is near where we live but is a ZPEP (that's a school with loads of violence)...

Esther I don't want to scare you or anything, but little white Babtous like you get blown away at my school, yo!

BLOWN UH-WAAAY!

This is him telling me

Hee hee

KLIK KLIK

What a jerk

... or try to get into a very posh free school in the centre of Paris by passing a test that's supposed to be super-difficult...

Which is what I did

The guy next to me was Portuguese or something

There were about 20 of us in one big room

No, this girl isn't my age — she's trying to get into Year 10

A man in a suit came in and gave us some papers. There was a short text with a few questions.

Year 7? Here...

I was in "I'm going to fail" mode. I was trembling

I... Yes, I...

The text told the story of a young couple who move to a different neighbourhood, but their dog Heinrich doesn't want to leave so it runs away from them and stays in the neighbourhood.

It was a Yorkshire terrier and apparently it was a bit full of itself

(I hate dogs. I prefer cats)

Then I read the questions and I couldn't believe how easy they were.

QUESTIONS
1) Is the couple elderly?
2) What is the dog's name?
3) What breed is it?
4) Does the dog want to move?
5) Imagine the rest of the story (two pages maximum)
....

I answered the questions and started to write the rest of the story as it came to me...

I want to be an editor when I grow up, so it was easy for me

Skrtch Skrtch

"Heinrich wanders around the neighbourhood. He's all alone. His owners have left. He's proud of himself."

I want to stay here. I can manage without them

"He doesn't know that eyes are observing him through a window."

"Night falls and he starts to feel hungry. Just then, he hears a soft voice calling him."

Oh, little lost doggie! Little doggie, are you hungry?

"Heinrich turns and sees a very beautiful young woman dressed in black. She smiles at him. She's holding a leg of smoked ham."

Come and taste this lovely ham, little doggie!

"Starving, Heinrich starts devouring the ham. 'What a great idea it was to stay here,' he thinks. The young woman tenderly pets him."

I love dogs! I'm going to call you Antoine after my brother... Eat! Eat more...

"But Heinrich's head is spinning... He's falling asleep..."

"When he opens his eyes, he's in a small cage in a basement. The sweet young woman's expression has changed. Her face is cold and harsh now. 'What's happening?' Heinrich wonders. 'I miss my owners. I should have gone with them...'"

Ah, awake at last, **ANTOINE**! I'd like to try a little experiment, just the two of us...

(Based on a true story told by Esther A, who is 11 years old)

Riad Sattouf

The Pipe-Cleaner Woman

Okay, so I'm going to continue with my story. I had two pages LMFAO (that's a rude way of saying LOL, in case you didn't know).

Me during the test, writing the rest of the story about Heinrich, an arrogant little dog who abandoned his owners

---

He is now the prisoner of the crazy young woman in black, who decides to punish him in the place of her hated dead brother...

BEG ME TO FORGIVE YOU FOR WHAT YOU DID TO ME, ANTOINE! OR I'LL SKIN YOU ALIVE!

Completely nuts

Weird horror — I love it

In the end, the woman is arrested and locked up and the dog is saved and returned to his former masters (although he now has only one ear because the crazy woman cut off the other one).

And so, the arrogant little dog learned his lesson

(I really hate dogs)

The boy next to me finished very quickly, and afterwards he dropped his phone twice. The third time he did it, the man in the suit who gave us the papers confiscated the phone and said:

Are you aware of where you are? And what you're doing here?

Hey it's not my fault.

Afterwards they picked up our papers and we went into a big, dingy room where we had to wait to be interviewed.

The ceiling was crumbling — look!

Mouldy

An hour later, a very nice (but extremely ugly) woman showed me into her office and asked me to read the story of the dog out loud.

"Heinrich the dog heard his masters calling him. But he didn't care: 'No, I'm not going to leave this neighbourhood,' he thought in his canine cerebellum"...

Body shaped like a pipe-cleaner

Then she asked me why I wanted to go to this school rather than the one near our home. I didn't dare tell her that we'd become poor since the birth of my little brother and that I didn't want to go to a ZPEP like my other brother because it had turned him into a moron.

Actually, um... well, basically your school is very famous and posh, so...

She didn't say anything. She wrote something down. Then she asked me what I wanted to do when I was older.

I want to be an editor of YA novels.

A writer?

No, editor.

Editor.

I want to... I'd really like to choose books based on my tastes and publish them. The writers would ask me to read them and I'd say, "It's good but put some more romance here, or more action there..." and so they'd end up being my books too, because I love reading. I read a lot.

She wrote something down. She asked me if I had a mobile phone. I said my dad wouldn't let me have one. And she said:

Good. He's quite right.

So the pipe-cleaner woman is ugly AND boring

And then something really weird happened. She put away her things, smiled, and said:

Tell me about your parents... What do they do?

The interview is over...

I almost lied and told her they did super-cool jobs (artist, fashion designer, etc.) but in the end I said, "My dad's a trainer at a gym and my mum works in insurance" (the truth, basically).

And who do you prefer — your father or your mother?

(Based on a true story told by Esther A, who is 11 years old)

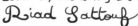

The Trap

So this is me answering some very personal questions about my family, asked by an extremely ugly woman who decides which students get into this super-posh free school and which don't

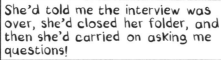

She'd told me the interview was over, she'd closed her folder, and then she'd carried on asking me questions!

You don't have any preference at all between your father and your mother?

Well, no!

Hmm...

Are they married?

I... um... yes...

Do they sometimes stop you doing things?

Well yeah, like everybody

"Like everybody?"

Like all parents...

What don't they let you do, for example?

I dunno, go out alone at night...

REALLY?

Well yeah... I mean, I'm only 11

11 isn't that young. Surely you can go out with your friends in the evening?

Well, no... I don't know...

I thought it was really weird that she was saying that. I realized she was trying to trap me into telling her the truth and that really stressed me out. I wanted to cry.

She was using a lie as bait to catch the truth

Do your parents tell you off sometimes?

You... You told me it was over...

Why did I say that?

When she opened the folder and wrote something down, I knew I'd blown it

You'll receive our response to your application by post at your address in the 6th arrondissement.

That is where you live, correct?

Did someone love this woman?

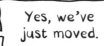

Yes, we've just moved.

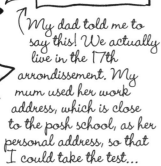

My dad told me to say this! We actually live in the 17th arrondissement. My mum used her work address, which is close to the posh school, as her personal address, so that I could take the test...

I cried soooooooo much when I saw my dad again...

DAAAD I'M SO SORRY I FAAAIIILED

I totally blew it

... AND YET, INCREDIBLE BUT TRUE, I WAS ACCEPTED!

My dad was so happy that I thought he was going to cry

This is the greatest day of my life

Making my dad happy is my favourite thing in the world

(Based on a true story told by Esther A, who is 11 years old)

Riad Sattouf

37

The List

I really like lists. I think they're very revealing about the person who makes them.

This is me making a list of things I find **BEAUTIFUL**

---

1. My dad's profile, backlit by the sun.

He looks like a god or a film star or something

---

2. The irises of my dad's eyes seen very close up.

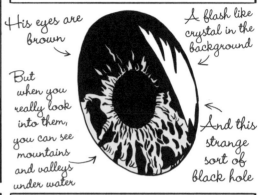

His eyes are brown

A flash like crystal in the background

But when you really look into them, you can see mountains and valleys under water

And this strange sort of black hole

---

3. The thickness of my baby brother's hair.

The exact colour of gold

Like, obscenely thick

He's only 8 months old and has no idea how lucky he is

---

4. Blue (the colour).

Joke photo taken on holiday

Like, whoa!

Me dressed all in blue in front of a blue sky

I look almost invisible

---

5. The aurora borealis (I've never seen it but apparently it's incredible).

If you don't know what it is, you can see it in the background of the poster for "Frozen" (an excellent Disney film)

It's this bit

REINE NEIGES

---

6. Gold (the metal and the colour).

My mum's jewellery box (which used to be my grandmother's)

Me trying on my mum's gold necklace (a bit too shiny)

I prefer matt gold

---

7. A woman in good make-up.

Do you recognize her? Yes, it's my mum!

The power of make-up, huh?!

---

8. All the different models of iPhones.

They're like useful jewellery

But I'm not allowed to have one

This is my dad's

---

9. The stars of "Chica Vampiro", a new comedy series about vampires that I really like.

Santiago Talledo

Greeicy Rendon

---

10. Modesty aside, I think I look very nice from behind.

My dad took this photo during our most recent holiday

HA HA!

JUST KIDDING!

(Based on a true story told by Esther A, who is 11 years old)

Riad Sattouf

The Beach

During our last holiday, we went to visit my grandmother in Bain-de-Bretagne (a town in Brittany with a strange name). It was good. One afternoon, we went for a walk on the beach in Saint-Malo (it's a really beautiful beach but there are too many dogs off the lead and that scares me). We were walking and I was thinking about how I'll soon have a brace on my teeth and I was worrying that it would make me ugly, etc. (you know, dark thoughts), when suddenly something really weird happened.

She disappeared towards the horizon and afterwards I wasn't scared of my braces any more or of getting old! **I SAW MYSELF IN THE FUTURE AND REALLY LIKED WHAT I SAW!**

(Based on a true story told by Esther A, who is 11 years old)

Riad Sattouf

The Improv Club

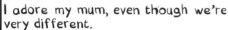

I adore my mum, even though we're very different.

This is me thinking that she's put on weight since my brother was born

My parents met when they were teenagers and they've been together ever since.

There's a photo of them looking really young on the fridge

The main thing I have in common with my mum is that we both adore my dad.

And how are my favourite ladies in the world this morning?

MWAH

He said "ladies", plural. I love him

Apart from that, she's much more "straight" than I am. Like, she works for a company that does "insurance" or something...

Our "premium serenity" contract covers ALL risks for your place of residence.

It sounds good!

It is good.

She says stuff like this all day long

Insurance is this thing that "protects"... For example, if there's a fire in your apartment, the insurance company pays you back for everything that's been destroyed. But in reality, before paying out, they try to find as many reasons as they can NOT to pay (like trying to prove you started the fire yourself — sneaky, huh?).

I'm sorry but we can't reimburse you. The "multi-risk" contract doesn't cover that risk.

How can she do that as a job? It's a mystery to me.

I'm more interested in "artistic" stuff than my mum is. She has no curiosity about music, for example.

I've already planned the names of our kids, our wedding date, I've already planned the classy ceremony on the beach, I'll drive an R8 and she can drive a Mini, we'll live on the 5th floor of a beautiful apartment near the Seine...

TURN THAT CRAP DOWN!

"Première fois" by Saub (I love this song)

My mum claims she's a bit artistic because she does "improv theatre". That means, like, sketches that you make up as you go along (good idea).

Next challenge: MIME!

Sometimes we go and see her at the club

The actors are given a subject and they have to invent a story.

The theme of the mime is "The beach!" Let's have a round of applause!

For example, my mum is pretending to arrive at the beach with her bag...

She sways her hips (to show she's playing a flirty, frivolous woman)

She's not at all like that when she goes to the beach

Then she mimes spreading out her towel.

I adore my mum, but honestly she's really bad at this

Moving her hands much too quickly

Anyone could do better if they really tried

It makes me ashamed to see her doing this stuff. My dad, on the other hand, thinks she's fantastic (good thing too, given they've been together for 20 years).

I wish I could teleport away from here

HA HA HA!

Here's a funny question: if my dad had been given the choice between my mum and me at the same age, who would he have chosen?

This is her pretending to read a crappy magazine on the beach

(Based on a true story told by Esther A, who is 11 years old)

Riad Sattouf

40

34 Years

My life has been horrible recently because I had two enormous zits...

This is me looking in the mirror and feeling totally depressed

... They were right next to each other ON MY NOSE.

Not only was this extremely ugly (and disgusting) but it really hurt too.

The pain woke me up at night and it felt like this →

TAK TAK

I'd had small zits before but nothing like this.

They were smaller, on my forehead, and they didn't hurt at all

–Hi...
–You look beautiful
–Thank you. You look beautifuller! I mean not fuller, you don't look fuller, but more beautiful
–Thank you

From "Frozen" (masterpiece)

I tried various "old wives' remedies" (like, secret tricks) to get rid of them.

Alcohol (nope)

Clay (useless)

Lemon juice (doesn't even burn) ↓

Toothpaste (excellent if you want your nose to smell minty)

Apart from that, useless →

I'm the ONLY ONE in my school to have zits like that. None of the boys have them.

You're pretty, yo... without zits!

HA HA

← Lucas, the most popular boy in school

They got bigger and bigger so my mum took me to the pharmacist, who had a foreign accent.

Oooh! Well, whatairver you do, don't burst thairm or you'll gairt scars! Heair, try this cream, it hairlps if you use it for 34 yeairs...

You hairve to put it on airvery day and wash your hands airfter...

I HAVE TO PUT IT ON FOR 34 YEARS?

?

HEX...

I tried to hold them back but tears welled in my eyes. I couldn't believe I'd have to use that cream for 34 years!

I said, "FOR DIRTY PORES, YAIRSS?" Sorry for my axcairnt!

Then my mum and the ugly foreign pharmacist laughed at me. But there was nothing funny about it. I just felt stupid now, as well as having two massive painful zits on my nose.

HA HA!

EXCAIRLAIRNT HA HA!

OSCILLO

I put the cream on and of course it didn't work. So I squeezed the zits and all this pus squirted out (gross, but that's life) and now it's better.

← In 34 years, I'll be 45 years old (!)

(Based on a true story told by Esther A, who is 11 years old)

Riad Sattouf

The Blow-up

So, this weekend, my mum and I had this huge blow-up. I get on pretty well with her, but we both have strong personalities...
Anyway, we all have a body, right? And we should be able to do what we want with it, right? And nobody else should get to
choose what we look like, right? You agree, right? Okay, so this has been going on for years, but I finally put a stop to it.
Let me explain: on Saturday evening, my mum came into my bedroom and said, as she usually does: "Your fringe is getting
long, I'm going to cut it." I looked her and I said: "You're not cutting anything! I don't want a fringe any more, okay? And
would you please knock before you come in my room from now on? Thank you." She didn't say anything. You should have
seen the look on her face! She was shocked! But, I mean, I don't go into her room and cut her hair, do I? Right?

After that, I gave myself the hairstyle I've wanted for years (but my mum wouldn't let me have)

I stuck the short hair from my fringe under the long hair, which I swept forward

I can almost do this kind of pose now

Needs to get a bit longer first

Stylish, right?

Looks different, right?

(I've got two huge zit scars on my nose – don't look, they're horrible)

How could I have walked round with a fringe all this time?

And I can still have a ponytail if I want – with a fresh twist

And when I'm in "antisocial" mode, I can put it like this so I don't see anyone

And it hides my zits too (except on my nose, sigh)

What will the kids at school think when they see me on Monday?

Hey, Esther's got rid of her fringe!

Wow, she's really changed lately

Yeah, she looks cool, yo

And if I sweep my hair back like this and put on make-up, I look really grown-up, don't you think?

(Based on a true story told by Esther A, who is 11 years old)

Riad Sattouf

Left and Right

If someone asked me, I'd say I was on the right.

This is me and my new hairstyle arriving at school →

Actually, I don't know anything about politics.

What will people think? (Not that I care, really) ↓

If you're on the right, it means that you're, like, in favour of people travelling, discovering the world, coming to live in our country and all that.

Ohh you're SO BEAUTIFUL
You really like it?
My best friend Cassandra ←

The right is... loving other people, even if they're not like us (like they don't have the same tastes or interests or whatever).

You look like a model on TV!
She changed her hair too, not long ago

Our mini-teacher (she's small so I call her mini-teacher – funny, right?) is on the right. She's obsessed by poverty and she's always telling us that we should "retribute wealth" or something.

Can anyone give me a definition of sustainable development?
I'm interested in the same things she is
We're both on the right

Being on the left is, like, the opposite. It's saying, "This is our country, go away," or, "This is mine, hands off!" to people in need (I just don't understand that kind of attitude).

Mathis, my secret love →
Développement durable

Being on the left is... what's the name of that woman who's always like, "Yeah Africans go back to Africa" etc.?

She's blonde and she's got really small teeth... and she doesn't like Rebeus (Arab people) or Renois (Black people). I'm the opposite – I think we should all mix together, like one big happy family!

YOUR NEW HARECUT TURNS ME ON ♥ LOLLLLL

But I don't know why everybody talks about "left" and "right". I heard on the TV that Francois Hollande was on the right (some protesters said that).

Hee hee Ha ha What's so funny?
Why are you laughing?

We're laughing at Esther and her new hairstyle, miss!
PFFF
SHE LOOKS LIKE RAPUNZEL, YO
My ex-friend Eugenie ←

I wanted to say to the teacher, you're supposed to be on the right, but laughing at other people's appearance is cruel and it's what people on the left do.

Come on now, calm down, Esther's hairstyle is very pretty
HA HA HA HA HA HAHAHA

Rapunzel   Me

What do you think?

(Based on a true story told by Esther A, who is 11 years old)

Riad Sattouf

43

Body Language

I have two brothers: Antoine, who's 15 years old (and I hate him because he's an idiot) and Gaetan, who's 9 months old (and I adore him, for now).

I wonder if there are any jobs where you get paid for observing babies and noting down your observations? I'd be pretty good at a job like that, I think.

At school, the teacher told us "We're not DESCENDED from monkeys, we ARE a type of monkey." Well, my brother is also a type of worm.

This is me in "experimenting on my baby brother" mode

Hff Gaah

I like testing how bendy he is

He's happy

The splits? No problem!

Goo

He just wriggles and rolls around

I'm really proud that I can do all the things he can do (which means bendiness is in our genes).

I enjoy this "physical and dynamic" dialogue that I have with him. It goes beyond language.

Actually I think he's fascinated by me (well, that's normal – I am his big sister).

I'm naturally supple

Well, I am a dancer (I go to dance class)

He watches me closely

Look how cute he is when he watches me roll across the floor

He can sit up and follow me with his eyes now.

What's funny is the emotions you can provoke in him, like, really easily.

If I move like this, he gets all stressed (LOL)

Hi there! Hi there!

I give a big smile

He smiles

Then suddenly I glare at him

?

GRRR

And then I smile...

Waaah

And he laughs while crying!

BOOO!

My mum doesn't really "kiffe" my experiments (for us young people, "kiffe" means, like, being really into something).

(Based on a true story told by Esther A, who is 11 years old)

Riad Sattouf

44

The Mummy Dog

The other night I had a dream about a giant mummy dog and her little puppies (whereas I HATE dogs in real life). Weirdly, I was asleep in my dream! I mean, I knew I was asleep.

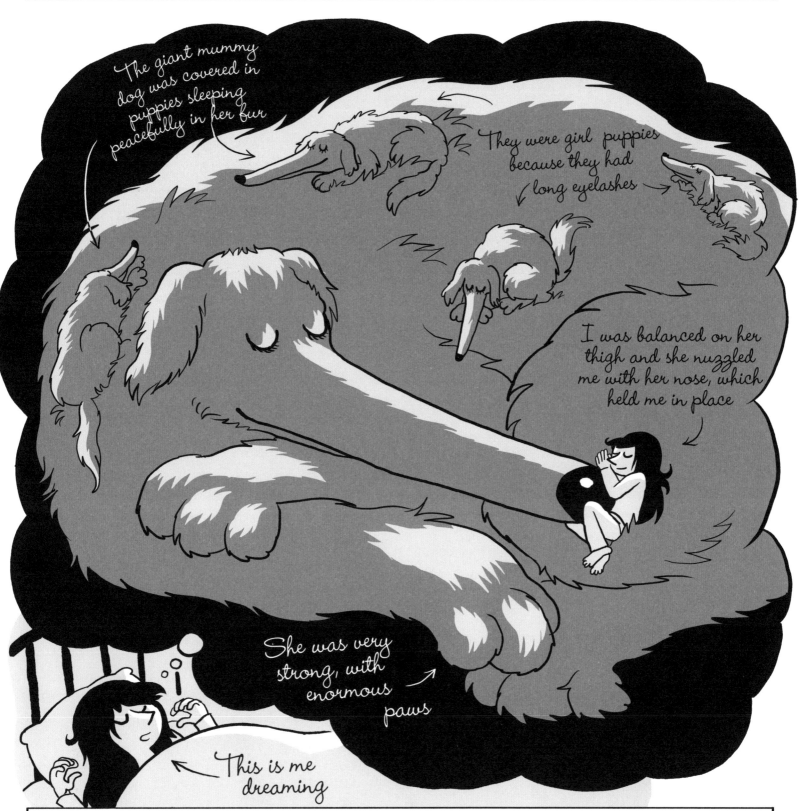

The giant mummy dog was covered in puppies sleeping peacefully in her fur

They were girl puppies because they had long eyelashes

I was balanced on her thigh and she nuzzled me with her nose, which held me in place

She was very strong, with enormous paws

This is me dreaming

It was a really sweet, cosy dream! And when I woke, I didn't hate dogs any more because I was in, "Wow, I wish I had a mummy dog" mode!

(Based on a true story told by Esther A, who is 11 years old)

Riad Sattouf

Rapping

I can't wait to be 18. Seriously. I'm counting the days. Time passes waaay too slowly.

When I'm 18, the first thing I'll do is leave this family and go away so I never have to see my brother again.

My parents will complain but I'll leave anyway.

I'll live in a tiny apartment with my friend Cassandra and we'll eat junk food all day and be happy.

I'll go out every night with my friends if I feel like it...

... or with my boyfriend.

The years will go by. The only one I'll see regularly is my dad. I'll have my dream job by then: editor of bestselling YA novels.

He'll weep with admiration at my incredible success.

Then will come the sad day when, after many years, my mum dies. And at her funeral, I'll see my older brother again.

Weakened by his endless failures, he'll try to patch things up with me.

She's my sister but I really detest her
I'm ashamed we share a common ancestor
I hope she cuts herself on a lemon zester
When she dies, I'll watch her corpse fester

When he dies, I'll pay for his gravestone. Well, not the whole thing (they're expensive) but the plaque that goes on top of it.

(Based on a true story told by Esther A, who is 11 years old)

Riad Sattouf

46

Bastille Day

My parents have gone to London for the weekend in "we're so in love" mode, my big brother has gone to stay with his friend Lucien (an idiot, just like him), and my grandmother has taken my little brother with her to Brittany. I stayed here for the weekend at my friend Cassandra's apartment. She lives in Saint-Denis (a town far away) but we went to see the Bastille Day fireworks in Paris at the Pont des Arts (it wasn't great – we couldn't see anything). We heard some teenagers say, "There's been an attack, it's really bad," so we wanted to look at Cassandra's phone but her mum confiscated it. Apparently what happened was really horrible but I don't know what it was because we didn't have time to see. Cassandra was really scared so when we got back to her room she said, "We have to build my dad's house." And I was like, "Huh?"

(Based on a true story told by Esther A, who is 11 years old)

The Secret of Cars

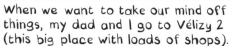

When we want to take our mind off things, my dad and I go to Vélizy 2 (this big place with loads of shops).

This is me and him in "let's buy stuff" mode

Hey, sweetie, you see that car in front? That's a Tesla... You don't see many of those, they're electric...

It's an American car

What do you mean, it's American?

Hang on, are you saying that not all cars are made in the same place?

I mean it's made in America! Our car's a Renault, it's French...

I must admit I'd never thought that cars could come from other countries! To be honest it's a subject I have, like, sub-zero interest in (LOL).

Seriously Esther? What did you think? That all cars just come from "the car factory"? They're like clothes, there are different brands...

FOR REAL, YO?

Baby, you know you're not supposed to say "yo" any more

It was bizarre. In fact I'd NEVER looked at cars before! So, did you know that there are Japanese cars called TSUSHI or something? We saw some!

They're tiny but quick

Even smaller in real life

And then there are German cars (Mercedes)...

They're, like, huge

Very old driver

Massive wheels

... Italian cars (Fiat Runto or something)...

Cube-shaped

Realistic drawing

... and English cars (Jaguar, like the animal!). Each country has its own brand.

But jaguars don't live in England...

That's not logical

WELL SPOTTED

My dad always says that our family isn't French but BRETON (the name for people from Brittany).

So are there Breton cars?

REALLY?

Of course! The famous Seagull 22

He told me that it was an amphibious car (that means it goes on water).

Brilliant idea!

... and you could sail it like a boat!

I want one when I'm older

Pure freedom!

In fact it was all just my dad's fantasy (that means a lie). But it really made me laugh!

I totally kiffe it when he says crazy stuff

HA HA

AND WHEN YOU HONK THE HORN IT SCREECHES LIKE A SEAGULL

♡ ♡ ♡ ♡ I LOVE HIM ♡ ♡ ♡ ♡

(Based on a true story told by Esther A, who is 11 years old)

Riad Sattouf

Prawns

Have you ever heard of these things called "prawns"?

This is me as a baby eating them

Yum yummm

My dad feeding me (look at his hairstyle)

Prawns are creatures that live underwater and that some people like to eat.

MORE PAWN

I loved them when I was little

But now I think they're the most disgusting things in the world.

The other day in the street I thought about how they tasted and I almost threw up

Bleurgh

Salty, soft, rubbery, gross

In fact, to me...

... a prawn and a cockroach <u>are the same thing, yo</u>

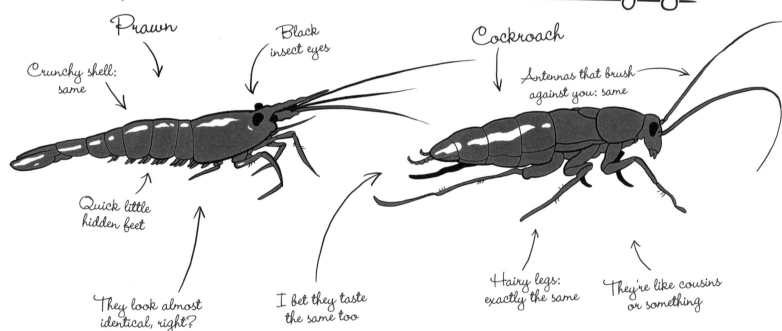

Prawn

Black insect eyes

Cockroach

Crunchy shell: same

Antennas that brush against you: same

Quick little hidden feet

They look almost identical, right?

I bet they taste the same too

Hairy legs: exactly the same

They're like cousins or something

Not only that but when you peel them they look like little caterpillars or worms...

Game: a worm has been hidden among these peeled prawns... Can you find it?

My dad adores them. When he eats them, he SUCKS THEIR HEADS.

MLMM

SLURP!

KKRNCH

MLMM

SLURP!

KKRNCH

(Based on a true story told by Esther A, who is 11 years old)

Riad Sattouf

49

The Wedding

Of course I DREAM of getting married one day, when I've become a grown-up.

This is me watching some Chinese newlyweds in the park near our house

A wedding is something that joins two lovers for eternity.

It's a sacred oath for all humans, wherever they're from

(even Chinese people)

You have to love each other and you must never cheat, because you both wear a WEDDING RING on one finger to remind you of your vows.

Gold rings that the bride and groom put on each other's fingers

The only thing I don't like about weddings is that the girl has to wear a white dress.

I'd wear trousers and a blouse with "explosive" coloured patterns because I think it's funny

I'd carry my bouquet like this (rebel bride, yo LOL)

Definitely high heels though

My future husband will be good-looking and thrilled by the idea of loving nobody but me until he dies.

Blond, why not? I love blond hair

He has to wear the traditional black suit and tie though (I'm the boss! Just kidding...)

I'd invite loads of people to my wedding. Family, friends, schoolmates...

They'll all be there to congratulate me

Even Eugenie

My parents and brothers

I've already been married twice before. But thankfully I got unmarried straight away each time.

I'm not going to join with someone for eternity when I'm just a kid

It was a "game"

WHOOOO

Divorce is a terrible tragedy that brings a marriage to an end. It's the death of love. I have some friends whose parents are divorced but who aren't upset about it. Worse, some of them are actually happy (Violette, for example).

Divorce is great! I have two homes now and I get twice as many Christmas and birthday presents!

My parents were married before I was born.

My mum wearing white, of course

My dad looking sooo handsome

I don't think I'd survive if my parents got divorced. I'm so scared of it. I think about it all the time when they argue, even just a little bit.

Don't add too much sugar to the cake this time...

Yeah well last time there wasn't enough!

But it'll be too sweet and you...

I LIKE IT WHEN IT'S...

You're not going to get divorced are you?

Then they look at me in "our daughter's crazy" mode and they smile

(Big relief – I was really worried)

(Based on a true story told by Esther A, who is 11 years old)

Riad Sattouf

50

The Betrothed

This week I dreamed that I was getting married! Probably because I was talking about weddings last week...

This is me just before the dream (I'd eaten too much ravioli)

I was in this really beautiful forest with loads of little super-cute furry animals around. They were leading me to my WEDDING.

HURRAH!

She's getting hitched!

This way, Esther!

Esther! Quick, to the altar!

After a while, I came to a clearing and I saw my husband waiting for me! I was super-happy because he was really good-looking (with wild, longish hair, like an art student or something)...

There he is! There he is, your BETROTHED!

I loved him immediately

I went over to him and then... OMG!

Um...

There you are, my love

Let's go to the altar

Yep, he was TINY!

I was panicking but I kept it hidden because this was my wedding and I didn't want to hurt his feelings. But I was thinking, "How can I spend eternity with such a small man?"

THEY'RE GETTING MARRIED!

YAAAY!

THEY'RE GETTING MARRIED!

The furry creatures were so happy

Afterwards we went to the house and the bed was cardboard and the pillows were paper and it was so enormous that we got lost in it.

So anyway, the next morning was weird... I was still looking for my husband... and I found my mum and my little brother sitting on the sofa reading a musical book for babies.

Press the button for the song!

Gooh

♪ He was a little man! He was a little man! And he had a funny house! ♪

The house was made of cardboard! The house was made of cardboard! The stairs were made of paper! The stairs were made of paper!

Come on Esther, sing with us! "He was a little man..."

(Based on a true story told by Esther A, who is 11 years old)

Riad Sattouf

Summer Camp

Just like last year, I went to a summer camp in Arcachon (a place near the sea).

This is me, Cassandra and my parents on the train station platform

I was so happy to be bringing Cassandra with me! We'd never gone anywhere together before.

We've always been in the same primary school but soon we'll be going to different secondary schools (so sad!)

We were going to make the most of this holiday!

We stood in front of the woman with the list of kids going to the camp, and then disaster struck!

Nope, sorry, there's no Cassandra on my list!

COKELI CAMP

So basically it was my mum who made the reservations on the internet and she messed up (typical her). I was the only one who could go.

Esther, yes. Cassandra, nope.

Are you kidding me?

Not at all!

She thought it was funny!

COKELI CAMP

Then Cassandra's mum just burst into tears and started yelling!

WHAAT?

Take her! Please!

I can't. We're full.

But what am I supposed to do? I have a job, I can't look after her!

TAKE HER!

I understand, madame, but she's not on the list. There's nothing I can do.

COKELI CAMP

The woman said the only way she could go was if someone else pulled out. So we waited. I got angry and shouted at my mum.

IF SHE DOESN'T GO, I'M NOT GOING, YO!

We watched people turn up one after another. It was like a nightmare.

Zinedine...

Yep, you're on the list!

Everybody had made their reservations correctly EXCEPT MY MUM.

I won't leave without you!

Hng! Hng!

After a while, Cassandra started trying to cheer me up!

Don't worry about me Esther! You should go...

Have fun...

At last it was time to leave. I thought I was going to die.

It's okay — one family didn't turn up. You can go.

COKELI CAMP

We hugged all the way to camp

(Based on a true story told by Esther A, who is 11 years old)

Riad Sattouf

52

The Tart

I have a very sweet tooth!

This is me eating sugar straight from the bag

GULP KRCH KRCH

In "addict" mode

That means like a "junkie"

It was raining the other day and my dad came back from Auchan with a surprise!

Look what I got you, sweetie!

MY FAVOURITE FOOD IN THE WHOLE WORLD!

Pfft they're not even in season! Why'd you buy that? It's bad for the planet, you know...

My mum the eternal killjoy

The strawberry tart of my dreams

The strawberries are big and firm and squeezed close together...

They look like jewels or something

Mmmm

I could live on strawberry tarts

... and covered in sweet, sticky, delicious juice

With a biscuity crust and lovely cream on top

And criss-cross designs on the side!

DAD: I LOVE YOU

When I'm grown up, I'll always have a strawberry tart in my fridge.

It'll be my consolation after a tough day at work

Nothing and nobody will stop me eating as much as I want.

I won't have to share it with anyone

KRNCH KRNNCH

KRRNCH KRNCH

I'll be an ADULT

And then I'll go to bed happy, thinking about my dad who used to give me tarts like that even out of season because he knew I loved them and his daughter's happiness was more important to him than the "fate of the planet" or whatever...

A tiny nostalgic tear will roll down my cheek (LOL)

(Based on a true story told by Esther A, who is 11 years old)

Riad Sattouf

Secondary School

Can you believe it? I've started secondary school at that free, posh place in the centre of Paris!

This is me in my bed, early in the morning on the first day of school, worrying about what it'll be like

I was afraid of being alone in the corridors of that enormous school, with nobody to help me find my classroom.

I was afraid of not being intelligent enough to understand the classes.

Esther? What's the answer? Didn't you learn anything in primary school?

$$z.12,45\sqrt{}\sqrt{x}b$$
$$(y) \times 45m.\cos$$
$$\frac{\sqrt{3},22 \times (b+c)}{\sqrt{3},22 \times (b+c)}$$
$$v+ab(73.5)$$
$$= ?$$

I was afraid the other children would be snooty aristocrats who'd look down on me.

Do you smell something?

Who's that commoner?

They let anybody in nowadays!

I was afraid of being the ugliest girl in a school full of models.

Just kill yourself or something

So I paid great care to what I wore.

Flowery outfit from England given to me by my aunt

So it still feels like summer

Light leather sandals

My dad took me by car (after that, I'll have to take a bus on my own). He was very happy.

There are ministers and presidents who went to this school, you know!

We arrived outside the building and my dad turned to me.

Okay, Esther, you're going to secondary school, so you're now allowed to have a phone.

HERE YOU ARE

FNAC

YAAAAAAAAY

FNAC

A NOKIA?

It's a very good TELEPHONE!

I'd received a letter telling me that I'd be in Class 6A. When I got to the school, I saw someone holding a sign. I didn't get lost. All the other students I saw were really ugly...

I felt less alone (LOL)

6A
Wait under this sign

... on the other hand, they all had an iPhone or a Samsung.

And when I say all, I mean **all**

6A
Wait under this sign

(Yep, even her)

(Based on a true story told by Esther A, who is 11 years old)

Riad Sattouf

54